THIS BOOK BELONGS TO

THE FLINTSTONES AND FRIENDS™ **ANNUAL** is published by Marvel Comics Ltd, 13/15 Arundel Street, London WC2R 3DX. **THE FLINTSTONES, TOP CAT, YOGI BEAR, WACKY RACES, SCOOBY-DOO, HUCKLEBERRY HOUND, QUICK DRAW McGRAW** and all other characters are trademarks of Hanna-Barbera Productions Inc. Copyright © 1977/1989 Hanna-Barbera Productions Inc.All rights reserved. Printed in Belgium.

HANNA-BARBERA'S THE FLINTSTONES CHRISTMAS PARTY

WHAT'S WRONG? YOU LOOK LIKE YOU JUST OPENED YOUR CHRISTMAS STOCKING AND FOUND A **FOOT** IN IT!

I DON'T KNOW, BARNEY... I JUST DON'T HAVE THE OL' CHRISTMAS SPIRIT!

FRED, WOULD YOU PLEASE GO DOWN TO THE POST OFFICE AND MAIL OUT THE PARTY INVITATIONS?

SURE, WILMA...

HE'S BEEN LIKE THAT FOR **DAYS** NOW!

LOOKS LIKE FRED'S GOT A CASE OF THE JINGLE BELL BLUES!

I DON'T GET IT! OTHER FOLKS ARE HAPPY... OTHER FOLKS ARE LOOKING FORWARD TO CHRISTMAS...

HEY, FLINTSTONE! TAKE A LOOK AT OUR CHRISTMAS DISPLAY! I'VE BEEN SETTING IT UP SINCE JULY 8!

TERRIFIC.

YULETIDE GREETINGS FROM THE GROSSROCK FAMILY

THE CHAMBER OF COMMERCE HAS A **BIG CASH PRIZE** FOR THE BEST CHRISTMAS DECORATION! I'M A **CINCH** TO COP IT!

THAT'S NICE.

BY THE TIME HE GETS TO TOWN, FRED IS NO MORE CHEERFUL....

I USED TO LOVE CHRISTMAS...WHAT'S HAPPENED TO ME?

HEY, MAC! HOW ABOUT SOME MONEY FOR THE BEDROCK ORPHANAGE?

MAYBE IF WE WENT OUT CAROLLING, THAT WOULD SNAP ME OUT OF IT...

THANKS! AND MERRY CHRISTMAS!

...BEDROCK ORPHANAGE...

THAT'S IT!

YABBA DABBA DOO! YOU JUST SAID THE MAGIC WORDS!

ALL I SAID WAS "MERRY CHRISTMAS!"

THIS IS TERRIFIC! STUPENDOUS!

I'M GLAD I DIDN'T WISH HIM A **HAPPY NEW YEAR,** TOO!

FRED RUSHES HOME AS QUICK AS HE CAN TO ASK...

"THE HAPPIEST DAY OF OUR LIVES?" I GUESS IT WOULD BE THE DAY WE ADOPTED BAMM BAMM!

PRECISELY!

THE DAY BEFORE CHRISTMAS, THE FINAL DELIVERY IS MADE...

YOU ARE SO KIND...

JUST SEE THAT SANTA GETS THE CREDIT!

WE'LL BE BACK LATER WITH MORE ORNAMENTS!

AH, BUT THERE'S A SURPRISE AT THE FLINTSTONE DOMICILE...

WILMA! WHAT ARE YOU DOING OUT HERE IN THE COLD?

WE'VE BEEN EVICTED FROM OUR OWN HOME!

HE SAID HE WAS FROM THE KRASS LOAN COMPANY!

WE'LL JUST SEE ABOUT THIS!

YOU HAVE NO RIGHT TO THROW US OUT OF OUR HOUSE... ESPECIALLY BEFORE CHRISTMAS!

HERE'S A COPY OF THE CONTRACT YOU SIGNED...AND A TICKET TO THE MOUNT ROCKWELL OBSERVATORY!

WHAT DO I NEED THIS TICKET FOR?

GO READ THE FINE PRINT!

SLAM!

Later, after a quick trip over to the observatory...

"...AND, IF LOAN IS NOT REPAID BY DECEMBER 24, KRASS LOAN COMPANY MAY SEIZE THE PROPERTY IN COMPENSATION!"

AND BACK AGAIN...

YOU CAN'T **DO** THIS! IT'S **CHRISTMAS EVE!**

SO IT IS! AND I FEEL GENEROUS! I'LL LET YOU STAY IN YOUR HOUSE **ONE** MORE DAY...

CHEER UP! YOU CAN **STILL** HAVE THE PARTY...

BOO HOO!

I HAVE A HANKY...

THAT'S RIGHT--THE PARTY IS TOMORROW! I DO HOPE ALL THE INVITATIONS ARRIVED IN TIME!

UH-OH!

I FORGOT TO...

WHAT'S "UH-OH?"

OH, ER...NOTHING! I'M GOING TO TAKE THIS LAST BOX OF DECORATIONS TO THE ORPHANAGE! ER...SEE YOU LATER!

ALL THE WAY OVER, FRED SAYS NASTY THINGS ABOUT FRED...

BEDROCK ORPHANAGE

YOU IMBECILE! YOU CHOWDER-HEAD! YOU REALLY BOTCHED THIS ONE UP, FLINTSTONE!

WHOOPS!

THAT **DOES** IT! I'M GOING HOME! EVERYTHING'S GONE WRONG!

BEDROCK ORPHANAGE

UNKNOWN TO FRED, HE IS BEING OBSERVED...

POOR FRED... HE'S DONE SUCH GOOD THINGS FOR THE ORPHANAGE...

"BEDROCK ORPHANAGE"

I EVEN FORGOT TO MAIL THE INVITATIONS TO OUR CHRISTMAS PARTY! NOW IT'S TOO LATE! WILMA WILL BE SO DISAPPOINTED!

IT'S **NEVER** TOO LATE AT CHRISTMAS TIME FOR GOOD THINGS TO HAPPEN! I'LL SEE TO IT THE FLINTSTONES ARE NOT DISAPPOINTED... EVEN IF I HAVE TO BRING THE GUESTS MYSELF!

BUT FIRST, THIS LITTLE TREE NEEDS A BIT OF **"IMPROVING"**... WITH MY MAGICAL TWINKLE DUST!

SO, WITH NOT SO MUCH AS A "HO, HO, HO," SANTA IS OFF AND AWAY...

AND AS HE GOES OUT OF SIGHT, THE LITTLE TREE CONTINUES TO GROW AND GLOW WITH THE SPIRIT OF CHRISTMAS!

13

SPIRIT IN THE SKY!

"Whooo-hooo! This is the life! Eh, Scoob?"

Shaggy grinned, sitting on a sandy bank, about to stuff his mouth with a giant hot dog.

A long, twisting tongue flicked out from Scooby Doo, wrapped itself around the hot dog and pulled it from Shaggy's grasp. Scooby swallowed it quickly.

"Rheah!" he giggled. "I love rholidays! Scooby Dooby Doo!"

The Gang had flown in to Miami, Florida, for a special well-deserved holiday from mysteries, and had spent the morning driving along the beautiful sun-drenched beaches of Florida Keys. Eventually they had arrived at Key Largo. First they visited the spectacular Coral Underwater Park, and then it was on to watch a special air display being held by the Red Devils display team.

"There's the aircraft now!" shouted Velma, standing up to watch the old-fashioned biplanes as they swooped out of the clouds to begin their display.

The field was packed with spectators who ooohed and ahhhed as the pilots performed their heart-stopping flying ballet.

"Eeep! You wouldn't get me up there!" gulped Shaggy, after watching a biplane spin towards the ground only to pull out of its dive at the last moment. "I get airsick standing on a chair!"

16

"Phooey!" laughed Fred. "I'd love to be flying one of those babies! They're fantastic!"

Daphne gave a sudden cry. "Look! There's another biplane – but it's got German markings and it's glowing . . . like a ghost!"

The new arrival seemed to upset the other pilots. The German Fokker D.7 swooped down towards the display team, guns blazing.

"It's attacking the display team!" gasped Fred.

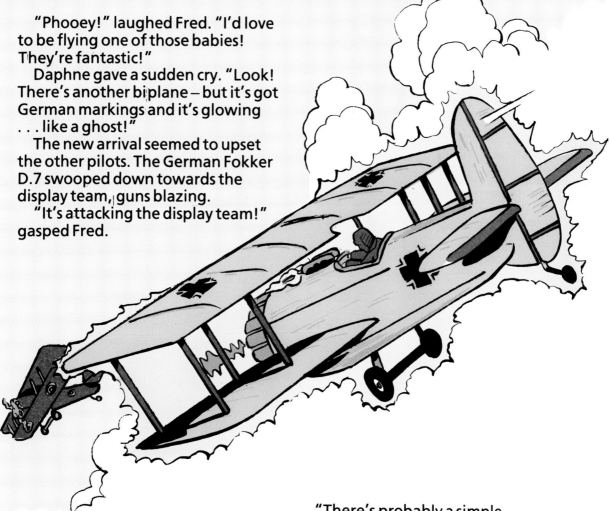

The Gang watched in astonishment as the pilots baled out and parachuted to earth. Their planes crashed safely into the sea. The ghostly intruder did a victory roll in the skies and then disappeared into a bank of cloud.

"Wow! Who was that guy?" cried Daphne. "And why did he attack those planes?"

"I don't know," said Velma, grimly. "But I think we've got a mystery to solve."

Scooby took one look at Shaggy. Then they both began to dig furiously at the sand trying to bury themselves.

"Rot me!" howled Scooby. "Rhis is my rholiday!"

"I'm with you, Scoob!" agreed Shaggy. "I'm not getting anywhere near that creepy pilot!"

"Don't be softies!" said Fred, pulling the timid pair out of the sand.

"There's probably a simple explanation for all this."

"Yeah, there's a simple explanation," said Big Jim Masters, the manager of the Red Devils. "That there was the ghost of Baron von Anvil, Germany's greatest fighter pilot of World War One."

"G-G-Ghost?" gurgled Shaggy, turning as pale as one.

"Sure is," went on Masters. "And out for revenge for getting shot down by my granddaddy back in 1917. He's attacked us twice now. Two of my bi planes are already wrecked. Much more of this and we'll go outta business."

But the display team's mechanic, Arnie Schwartz, disagreed. "You ask me, Masters is behind all this," he scowled later, hammering at the engine of a biplane with a large spanner. "He's hired someone to wreck the team so he can collect on the insurance."

"What do you think?" asked Velma later, when the gang held a conference. "Is it really a ghost, or just a confidence trick?"

Fred smiled. "You know what we do when we don't know the answers – let's investigate!"

Shaggy groaned. "I was afraid you were going to say that!"

"Ree too!" whimpered Scooby.

Jim Masters showed the Gang around the airfield. "The biplanes we use are old crop-dusters," he explained. "They're called biplanes because they have two sets of wings held together by wing struts and stays." He pointed to the rods and wires between the wings.

"Our pilots sometimes climb out of the cockpit and perform stunts on the wings," went on Masters. He looked at Shaggy. "You seem the brave type. Do you fancy 'walking the wing'?"

Shaggy's knees began to shake and knock. "Neep! Blurp! Gurrrf!" he gurgled.

"I think that means, no thanks!" laughed Daphne. "Now if you don't mind, Mr Masters, I think it's time we did some investigating. Come on, gang!"

"I know where we should start looking, Scoob," grinned Shaggy, winking at his best friend. Scooby chuckled and followed, his tongue slurrrping hungrily.

"Rood!" he barked happily as they entered the small kitchen at the back of the aircraft hanger. "Rh'm starving!"

"Me too!" laughed Shaggy, pulling open the fridge door. "And Mr Masters did say to help ourselves to anything we wanted. So one double-triple-quadruple decker salad roll coming up!"

The roll completed and spilling over with its filling of tomato-cucumber-onion-lettuce-radish-and-mushrooms, the friends were about to tuck in when the door burst open . . . and there stood a glowing white man in an ancient German pilot's uniform.

"Gulp! B-Baron von A-Anvil, I presume!" quaked Shaggy, and then, "Let's get outta here, Scooby Doo!"

Since the ghostly German pilot was blocking the one way out Scooby did what any sensible dog who was scared stiff would do. He dived through the open window, quickly followed by Shaggy.

"Re've got to ride!" wailed Scooby, running around the airfield.

"We can hide in here, Scoob!" said Shaggy, scrambling into the cockpit of one of the biplanes, and pulling Scooby Doo behind him.

The biplane's engine was already running, as if it were to be taken out for a test flight. So when Scooby tried to turn around in the cramped cockpit and accidently pushed down on the throttle lever the boys had the fright of their lives.

"Yeeeeooooow!" screamed Shaggy. "We're moving!"

The plane lurched along the runway. And that's all it would have done if a frightened Shaggy hadn't pulled back on the control stick. But he did and the plane took off into the air!

"Rhaggy!" whimpered Scooby, hiding his eyes behind his paws, not daring to look. "Re're taking off!"

The bi plane swiftly gained height. Shaggy pushed the control lever the other way – and the plane dived towards the ground.

"Yaaaaarrrrgggghhh!" screamed Shaggy and Scooby together.

Zooooom! The plane just missed crashing into the aircraft hanger, then it swooped up into the air again.

"How do we get down?" screamed Shaggy. Then he saw the ghostly white shape of the Fokker D.7 in front of them.

"Oh, no! Baron von Wotsisname has come to haunt us even up here!"

The Fokker twisted in the sky after its prey. Shaggy pulled on the control stick again . . . did a loop the loop . . . and Scooby fell out of his seat!

"Raggy!" he cried, catching hold of one of the wing struts. Poor Scooby found himself hanging from the wing.

Shaggy tried to reach his friend to save him. Then the Fokker attacked again. "Hold on, Scoob!" shouted Shaggy, turning out of the Fokker's path.

But Scooby lost his grip! "Goodbye Raggy!" he cried, spinning out of the sky. Then flumph! He landed safely in the cockpit of the Fokker on top of the ghostly German.

"Get off, Mutt! I can't see!" growled the pilot, who didn't sound German at all. But Scooby was too scared to let go. The pilot had to land the plane or risk crashing.

"Geep! Ranks for the ride!" quivered a shaken Scooby as he flopped out of the cockpit into the arms of Fred. The police had already arrived. And so had Shaggy, who had managed to crash his plane in the sea and swum safely to shore.

The German pilot was pulled out of the plane. Fred tore off the ghostly mask to reveal . . .

"Arnie Schwartz!" gasped Daphne.

"Yeah, it was me!" growled Schwartz. "I was paid to put Masters outta business by a rival display team! I used blanks when I attacked them before! I was doing well too — until that stoopid mutt got in my way!"

After Schwartz had been taken away the friends stayed to see the display team in action. But it was Scooby who won first prize for 'walking the wing'!

"We'll have to catch our own plane soon," said Fred, looking at his watch.

Shaggy hurried away, Scooby following him. "Er, we'll walk if you don't mind!" he said, looking a sickly green.

"Rheah! Ralk!" agreed Scooby, chuckling. "Scooby Dooby Doo!"

THE END

20

THE **SPOOKY TREE!**

IS FULL OF

MONSTERS!

SCOOBY-DOO

HAS SPOTTED TEN

OF THEM!

How about you? This game of hide and seek ends on page 61.

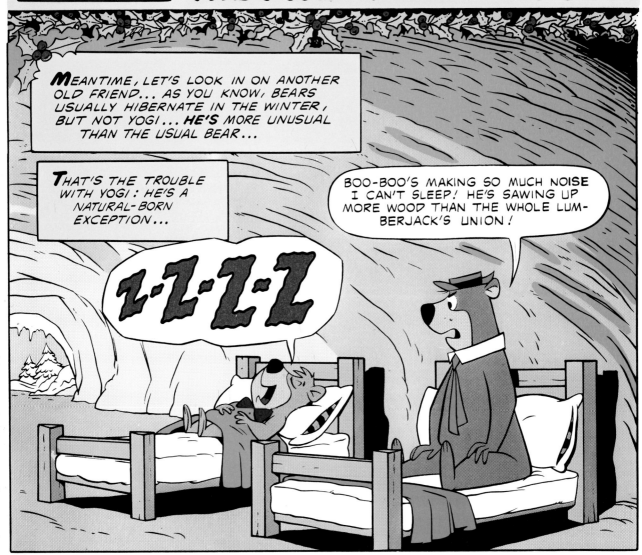

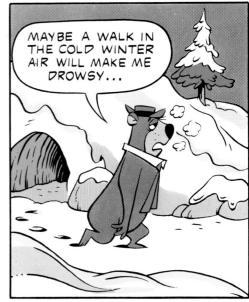

Z-Z-Z-

OUT, OUT, **OUT!**

MAY SANTA BRING YOU A YEAR'S SUPPLY OF INDUSTRIAL. **SMOG** FOR CHRISTMAS!

COMPARED TO **HIM,** EBENEEZER SCROOGE WAS "MISS CONGENIALITY!"

SO MUCH FOR OUR NICE, PEACEFUL WINTER--!

ARE YOU SURE? WELL, WE'VE GOT THE NORTH SECTOR MAPS HERE...WE'LL HAVE A LOOK AROUND!

WE'VE GOT A LOST BOY... FOUR-FOOT-EIGHT, ABOUT EIGHTY POUNDS! LOOKS LIKE A RUNAWAY!

GO GET THE SNOWMOBILE!

MEANWHILE ON THE OUTSIDE...

MIGHT AS WELL HEAD BACK! I GUESS I'LL JUST HAVE TO LIVE WITH BOO-BOO'S SNORING!

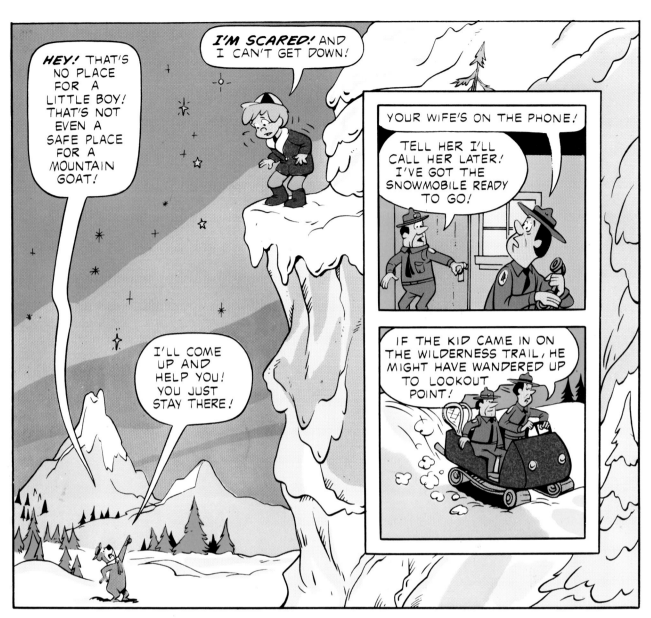

SHORTLY...

WAKE UP! MR. RANGER WANTS US TO COME SHARE CHRISTMAS WITH HIM!

MKSLPH? SMGPHRTH!

... BEFORE THAT, YOGI, **I'D** LIKE TO TAKE YOU TO THE FLINTSTONES' CHRISTMAS PARTY! I'LL HAVE YOU BACK IN TIME TO VISIT RANGER SMITH!

SANTA CLAUS!

WHY'D YOU WAKE ME UP, YOGI?

COME ON, BOO-BOO! SANTA CLAUS IS TAKING US TO A CHRISTMAS PARTY!

CLIMB ABOARD MY SLEIGH, FELLOWS! DESTINATION: **BEDROCK!**

SANTA HEADS SKYWARD, AND IN A HOME NOT FAR AWAY...

OH BOY! A BASEBALL BAT! ...AND A MITT! ...AND...

IT'S SO GOOD TO HAVE YOU HOME, DARLING...

AND BELIEVE ME, I'LL BE HERE EVERY CHRISTMAS FROM NOW ON, DEAR!

AMAZING BEAR!

Yogi Bear can sniff out a pic-a-nic basket a mile away! Help him find his way through the Jellystone maze to the goodies! Yes indeedy!

START

Yogi watch out! Ranger Smith is about!

PIT-STOP AT HOT ROCK!

Yes folks! You've joined us just in time as the world's wackiest racers roar off across the rugged ruins of Ringadingaling, New Jersey!

And it's the Ant Hill Mob careering into the lead with their car being led by the Mob themselves. Leader Clyde has tied a giant dog's lead around the Mob and making them pull Number 7 like huskies.

"Mush, you guys!" barks leader Clyde, whacking his men on the head with a whip. "If we saves the gas now, we won't have ta make a pit stop at Hot Rock like dem other mugs!"

Following close behind is Red Max in Number 10, the Crimson Haybailer, and hot on his tail is the Buzz Wagon.

"Zay! Don't get zo close!" cries Max, as the Buzz Wagon's saw-teeth wheels zip through the tail-end of the Crimson Haybailer, and Max finds himself at the end of the tale without a tail!

"Zis is zo embarrizing!" cries Max, turning his plane-car off the road, and then running back to pick up its tail. "Vere is zer doctor ven you needs vun!"

Rufus Ruffcut waves goodbye to Max and pours on the heat to push the Buzz Wagon towards his next victim. "Hur! I'll cut up the next racer too!" he chuckles.

But Rufus' foul plan falls foul of the Slag Brother's Boulder Mobile whose stone frame smashes the teeth of the Buzz Wagon's saw-teeth wheels.

"Hey! Ya cheats!" cries Rufus as his car swerves off the road and ends up in a ditch.

"Ugggh! Gruggg!" chuckle the brothers Slag, bopping each other on the bonce with their clubs, which means "Well done!" in caveman language.

And here's Dick Dastardly in Double Zero, the Mean Machine. Or is it?

"Snaffa! Crassin! Frassin!" snarls Dick behind the wheel of his souped-up special. Which means, of course, that it isn't tricky Dickey at all, but his dog Muttley, dressed up as Dick.

So where's Dirty Dastardly and what's he up to? He's way ahead of the field, setting up another dirty trick.

"How true!" beams Dick, hiding behind a rock. "Muttley's dressed as me so the others don't find out what I'm up to. I've set a giant spring under the road. When the first car drives over it, the spring will catapult it into the air where it will drop on the other racers smashing their cars to itsy-bitsy pieces! Then I'll win the race! Heh, heh! I'm such a rotter!"

And here comes the first car now! Oh no! It's pretty Penelope Pitstop in the Compact Pussycat. Look out, Penny!

"Wah, hello Sugar!" waves Penny, busy looking in her compact mirror while she makes up her face. Then **twannng!** Dastardly's dastardly spring springs up under her and her car goes flying high into the air.

"Whooo-hooo! This is a gas!" giggles Penny, looking down at the ground far below.

"Har, har! I can't wait to hear the crash!" laughs Dick Dastardly. "There's going to be a big wreck any minute!"

Crasssssshh! Dick's right. There is a crash – but not where he expected it. Instead of crashing onto the other cars, the Compact Pussycat lands on Dick instead, flattening him neck-deep into the desert floor. Boy, does he looked wrecked!

"Glunk!" gasps Dastardly. And don't worry, folks. Penny's suspension is so strong she bounces off the ground and into the lead!

The Double Zero pulls up at the spot where Dick is in a spot of bother.

"Snaffa! Crassin! Frassin!" growls Dick. Or is it Muttley? No, this time it really is Dick, up to his neck in trouble – and sand – again. "Muttley! Save me!" he yells.

"Heh! Heh!" sniggers Muttley, who brings a bucket and spade out of the Mean Machine so that he can build a few sandcastles before he rescues his boss.

Without Dastardly to foul the trail, the Wacky racers are making headway towards the Hot Rock Pit Stop. First to sight the fill-up station is Sarge and Meekly in Number 6, and Army Surplus Special.

"Meekly! Target sighted!" bellows the Sarge. "Attack!"

"Right, Sarge!" says Meekly, meekly. He turns the tank's turret backwards and fires! The force of the explosion blows the Surplus Special across the desert floor – and unfortunately past the filling station.

"Meekly! Stop!" yells the Sarge.

"Gee, Sarge! I can't!" wails Meekly. Then he smiles. "But don't worry. We'll stop in a second."

"Why?" asks the Sarge.

"We're about to collide with that there cliff, Sarge!"

Kaa-Boooooom!

While Number 6 dig themselves free of the cliff we find that Professor Pat Pending in his Coverta-Car has reached Hot Rocks first.

"I wonder why they call it Hot Rock?" he says, frowning.

He leaps out of the car to fill up and leaps up instead. "Yeeeeooow! The rocks on the ground are red hot!" he squeals, leaping back into Number 3, hot-foot.

And watch out for your tyres, Professor! The ground's so hot, they're melting!

"Action stations!" shouts the Prof. He pushes one of the buttons on the car's control panel and converts it into a heli-car-pter. With rotor blades whirling, Number 3 lifts off the ground. Then the Professor hooks the pump gun with a fishing rod and fills up in the air!

"No problem!" chuckles Pat Pending, and flies off to find the finishing line.

"Huh! I've missed one, but I'll get the others!" snarls Dirty Dick.

You'd better be quick, Dick. The others are making tracks to the fill up spot to have a spot of filling up!

Dick fills up the Double Zero double quick with petrol. But how come his feet don't get hot?

"I'm wearing my 'foot-freezer' snowboots, of course!" cackles Dick. "They keep my tootsies nice and cold, no matter how hot it gets! Muttley! Bring the explosives!"

Explosives? Dick, what dirty devilment are you doing?!

"Heh! I'm going to blow up the petrol pumps. Then there'll be no fuel for the other cars and they'll never be able to reach the winning line! Oooooh! I love me – I'm so … so …"

Dastardly?

"Exactly!" beams Dick. "I'm so glad you agree! Hurry up, Muttley!"

Muttley jumps out of the car with the box of gelignite – high explosives! But he's not wearing shoes, and the hot rocks are hot on his poor paws.

"Grrrroooouuucch!" he yelps, jumping back and dropping the box. The gelignite falls out and rolls towards the petrol pumps.

"Muttley! You dumb mutt!" cries Dick in a panic. "The rocks are so hot they'll make the explosives explode!"

Boooooooooommmmmm! The explosion is so large it rips out the entire ground from the petrol pumps. The pumps fly through the air and land safely in front of the other cars.

"Wahooooo!" yells Hillbilly Luke in the Arkansas Chugabug. "Dagnab it! That Dastardly yokel has done us a favour! We's got our gas without getting hot feet!"

"And now we're on the last stretch home!" cheers Peter Perfect in the sleek-slick Turbo Terrific. "Most kind of Dick. I must remember to thank the chappie later – wherever he is!"

Yes, where is he? Where he had stood there is now only a big hole! Has Dick been blown to itsy-bitsy pieces?

At last, the racers are roaring towards the finish! Who will it be? The desert dust is hiding the cars from the spectators but here comes – good grief! It's gorgeous Penny Pitstop passing the finish line first, followed by Red Max, in the patched up Crimson Haybailer and in third place it's the Slag Brothers! What a race!

Suddenly the ground is rocked by a loud crash. Everyone looks back before the finishing line to find a smashed-up Mean Machine, surrounding a blackened Dastardly and Muttley. The explosion has blown them so high into the air they've only just landed!

"Boy, this race ended with a bang!" laughs Peter.

"Bah!" is all Dick has the strength to say!

THE END

DICK'S DASTARDLY

Dirty Dick Dastardly is in a bad mood after losing the big race. So he's set a really devious puzzle for you to solve! Curses! Hidden on the page opposite are the names of many of your favourite Hanna-Barbera characters. How many can you find? Here's Dick to tell you all the names in the puzzle...

WORD SEARCH!

CHRISTMAS OUT WEST... THOUGH YOU'D NEVER KNOW IT FROM THE WEATHER. EXPECTED HIGH: IN THE SEVENTIES. EXPECTED SNOW: NONE WHATSOEVER...

♪ OH, JINGLE BELLS! JINGLE BELLS ♪

SHERIFF

I SHORE DON'T FEEL TOO PRETTY GOOD!

I KNOW! QUEEKSTRAW... HIS SINGING, SHE HAVE THE SAME EFFECT ON ME!

C.I., I DON'T MEAN THAT! SHUCKS, IT'S A HOOT AND A HOLLER BETTER'N MY SINGIN'! I WAS TALKING ABOUT HOW THERE'S NO SNOW!

YOU ARE SORRY YOU CAME TO SPEND CHRISTMAS WITH US, HUCK?

CAN'T LET 'EM THINK I'M NOT HAVING A GOOD TIME...

OH, I'M VERY GLAD, BABA LOOIE! VERY GLAD, INDEEDY!

WELL, THAT'S GOOD TO HEAR!

37

39

HOW MANY WORDS CAN YOU FIND IN...

HUCKLEBERRY HOUND

HUNDREDS PROBABLY!

But we'll let you off with, say, 35 words (each word containing no less than 4 letters).

List your words here:

REEL

CORK

Check you answers against ours on page 61.

CHAPTER FOUR

A VERY MERRY TOP CAT

THERE'S PLENTY OF REAL SNOW IN TOWN-- SO MUCH SO THAT TOP CAT AND COMPANY DECIDED TO MAKE SOMETHING OF IT...

NO, NO, *NO!* YOU CAN'T BUILD A SNOWMAN ON A PUBLIC STREET!

BUT, OFFICER DIBBLE...

CLANK!

YEOWTCH!

YOU CATS CAUSE ME MORE TROUBLE!

COME, GANG--LET'S BEAT A HASTY RETREAT! AND THE HASTIER, THE BETTER!

"... AM ARRIVING ON FLIGHT 303 AT NOON, ANXIOUS TO SEE YOU..." AND IT'S SIGNED *YOUR MOTHER!*

BENNY'S MOTHER'S COMING TO TOWN? LET'S SEE IF WE CAN CATCH HIM!

TOO LATE! HE'S PROBABLY HALF-WAY OUT OF TOWN BY NOW!

SUBWAY

WHAT DO WE DO NOW?

"WHAT DO WE DO NOW," HE ASKS! WE PICK HER UP AT THE AIRPORT, THAT'S WHAT WE DO! LET'S GO!

A QUICK PROMENADE TO THE AIRPORT, AND...

YOU MUST BE SPOOK... AND YOU'RE CHOO CHOO... AND FANCY FANCY... AND BRAIN... AND OF COURSE, YOU'RE TOP CAT!

YOU'RE PROBABLY WONDERING WHERE BENNY IS! YOU SEE...

OH, I KNOW WHY HE ISN'T HERE! HE'S BUSY RUNNING HIS CORPORATION!

ER... HIS **WHAT**?

HE WROTE ME MANY TIMES ABOUT HIS SUCCESS -- HIS MANSION, HIS BUSINESS... I'M **SO PROUD** OF BENNY!

SO **THAT'S** WHY HE LEFT TOWN, FELLAS! HE KNEW HIS MA WAS COMING AND HE COULDN'T FACE HER AFTER ALL THOSE FIBS!

IF SHE FINDS OUT THE TRUTH, IT'LL BREAK HER HEART!

SHE **WON'T** FIND OUT! GUYS, GO INTO TOWN AND TELL ALL OUR PALS TO PLAY ALONG!

OKAY, MOTHER BALL! SHALL WE BE OFF?

OH, YES! I CAN'T WAIT TO SEE HOW SUCCESSFUL MY DEAR BENNY IS!

WHILE THE GANG SCATTERS TO SET THINGS UP...

BENNY'S COMPANY IS IN **THAT** HUGE BUILDING?

HEAVENS, NO! THAT'S JUST HIS **MAIL ROOM**!

THEY KEEP TRACK OF THE DIFFERENT **POST CODES** IN HIS **BIG** BUILDING!

THANKS, OFFICER DIBBLE! I FEEL LIKE A VERY MERRY TOP CAT!

MERRY CHRISTMAS, TOP CAT!

...BUT, YOU KNOW, I'D BE PROUD OF MY SON IF HE *WEREN'T* WEALTHY!

I'M GLAD TO HEAR YOU SAY THAT, MA -- I HAVE A CONFESSION TO MAKE...

BENNY THE BILLIONAIRE IS A *FAKE!*

BENNY!

AND SO, BENNY SPILLS OUT THE TRUTH TO HER AND...

I'M GLAD HE'S HONEST -- AND POOR OR RICH, HE'S *MY SON!*

HOW ABOUT *THAT!* AFTER ALL WE WENT THROUGH, SHE'S GLAD HE'S *POOR!*

I HAVE TO CATCH MY PLANE HOME! GOOD-BYE, BENNY! GOOD-BYE, TOP CAT!

GOOD-BYE, MA!

I HAD TO TELL HER GUYS...BUT THANKS FOR WHAT YOU TRIED TO DO!

WE UNDERSTAND, BENNY!

LET'S GET ON WITH OUR CHRISTMAS PARTY! IT SEEMS LIKE A *MILLION YEARS* SINCE OUR LAST ONE!

FUNNY YOU SHOULD MENTION *A PARTY,* TOP CAT...

COLOUR! with DIBBLE!

Oh no! The sarge has ordered Officer Dibble to colour in this picture of Top Cat and his pals in double-quick time! Poor Dibble is far too busy. . . Why don't you get some felt tipped pens or crayons and give him some help?

Whoops! One of Top Cat's gang is missing from the picture! Which one is it? Answer on page 61.

CHAPTER FIVE

THE HAPPIEST DAY OF ALL

IT WAS THE MOST BEAUTIFUL OF CHRISTMAS MORNINGS IN BEDROCK...

...BUT FRED DIDN'T SLEEP SO WELL. HE KEPT THINKING ABOUT THE CHRISTMAS PARTY HE MUFFED...

ACROSS TOWN, A JUDGING COMMITTEE WAS IN AWE OF A SINGLE TREE THEY HAD COME ACROSS...

THEY'D BEEN STARING AT IT FOR THE BETTER PART OF AN HOUR BEFORE SOMEONE FINALLY SAID...

...THIS IS THE MOST BEAUTIFUL THING I'VE EVER SEEN IN MY WHOLE LIFE!

BEDROCK ORPHANAGE

THE TREE THAT SHONE WITH THE SPIRIT OF CHRISTMAS... THAT WAS WHAT THEY COULD NOT TAKE THEIR EYES OFF...AND WITH GOOD REASON.

51

52

53

DRAW FRED!

YUP, YOUR CHANCE TO BECOME A GREAT CARTOONIST! (WELL, IT'S A START!) SIMPLY COPY THE DRAWING ON THE LEFT HAND SIDE OF THE PAGE. USE A PENCIL AND KEEP TRYING TILL YOU GET IT RIGHT, THEN COLOUR IT IN!

FRED HAPPY!

FRED UNHAPPY!

YOGI'S NEW YEAR!

A loud snoring came from a cave in Jellystone Park. The snoring was so loud, it shook the snow from the trees.

Inside the cave, Yogi Bear, and his best friend, Boo-Boo, were hibernating. At least, they were, until there was a loud crack, and their ceiling fell in, under the heavy weight of snow.

Flumpphh! The snow landed right on top of Yogi!

"Hallp! The Ab-bon-bon-ible Snowbear's got me!" he cried, leaping out of bed.

Yogi's cries woke Boo-Boo. "It's not a monster, Yogi! The snow's brought down our old ceiling."

Boo-Boo clambered out of bed. He spent the morning fixing a large wooden door across the hole to keep out the snow and cold. Yogi didn't feel like working after his fright, so he sat and supervised.

"Right, Yogi, all fixed," said Boo-Boo, climbing back into bed. "Now let's go to sleep. I'm tired!"

"I can't sleep now," groaned Yogi. "My tummy's groaning. It's hungry. It needs a pic-a-nic basket full of goodies to eat!"

Boo-Boo wasn't listening. He was already fast asleep.

"Humph!" snorted Yogi, leaving his cave, and tromping off around Jellystone Park in the deep snow. "There must be a stray pic-a-nic basket around here somewhere. Even a half-full one will do. I'm a hungry bear and I don't care!"

Much to Yogi's disappointment, there wasn't a picnic basket to be found. "Bah! Humbug! And Scrooge-like grumbles!" moaned Yogi, sitting down for a rest. "This park is empty of my favourite animal — the common or garden vis-it-or! They must all hibernate like bears do!"

He was about to return, empty tummy, to his cave, when the delicious aroma of cooked food drifted under his nose.

"Hmmm! I do declare! There's food for Yogi Bear!"

Yogi followed the smell, until he arrived at the Park's Ranger Station. Looking through a window, Yogi could see a room decorated with Christmas tinsel. Much more important, there were six tables laid out with all manner of mouth-watering party food.

"Yo! Ho! Ho! Ranger Smith must be having guests!" beamed Yogi. "And I shall be one of them!"

Bang! Bang! Bang! went Yogi's fist on the door. **Bang! Bang! Bang!** it went again, only this time on Ranger Smith's head, as he opened the door.

"Yeeoowch! Yogi! What do you think you're doing?" shouted the Ranger.

Yogi explained all about his collapsed roof and hungry tummy. "So, if you could lend your kind heart to spare a morsel or two for a weary and starving bear, it would be most appreciated, like," grinned Yogi.

"You must be joking!" spluttered Ranger Smith. "This food is for the New Year's Eve fancy dress party I'm holding tonight. It is not for bears who should be hibernating! Now go back to your cave, Yogi, and don't disturb me again!"

With that, the Ranger slammed shut the door in Yogi's face.

"Of course, we both know," smiled Yogi, "t the Ranger's only playing a jest on me! He wants to feed me really – so I'll join in his game!"

He hurried around to the back of the Ranger Station. "Here's a window that doesn't catch properly," beamed Yogi, pulling the window up. "All I have to do is climb in, help myself to a titbit or three, and leave a thank-you note for kind Ranger Smith."

But Yogi's problems started before he even got inside.

"Urrumpph! Stupid window must have shrunk since I used it last!" he complained, struggling to pull his fat body through the small opening. When Yogi was half-in, but still half-out, he found he couldn't move, forwards, or backwards!

"Yipes! Help! Bear in distress!" he cried. "I need Ranger-type assistance, pronto-like!"

Ranger Smith came in the room to see what all the noise was about. "Yogi! What do you think you're doing?"

Yogi looked ashamed at being caught. "Um, cleaning your windows?" he asked, hopefully.

Ranger Smith went outside, grabbed hold of Yogi's legs, and pulled. Plop! Yogi tumbled free of the window, and landed in the snow.

"Phew! Saved!" he cheered. "Thank you, Ranger Smith, my saviour! My hero!" Then Yogi frowned. "Ranger Smith? Hello?" He looked all around where he was sitting. Ranger Smith was nowhere to be seen.

"Aha! He's playing hide-and-seek with his favourite bear!" chuckled Yogi. "Now I wonder where he could be?"

"Mmmmph! Grrlumphh! Mmmurrgh!" came a muffled voice under where Yogi was sitting.

Yogi stood up. Lying at his feet, flattened deep in the snow, was a very cross Ranger, who had been knocked over when Yogi landed on him.

"Yo-Ho-Ho! Caught you!" said Yogi, still thinking he was playing a game. "What shall we play next?"

"We're not playing anything!" roared Ranger Smith. "If you're not back in your cave in ten seconds, I'll…I'll…!"

Yogi decided to retreat. "I won't disturb the Ranger again! I'll just help myself to some food and be on my way!"

Reaching his cave, Yogi searched in this toy box until he found his old bow and sucker-tipped arrow set.

"Heh! I won't have to step one foot inside the Ranger Station with this!" he chuckled.

He tied a long piece of rope to the end of an arrow, and then made his way back through the snow to the Ranger Station.

The Station door was shut. Picking up a large stone, Yogi threw it at the door.

58

It bounced off with a loud knock! Yogi ducked behind a bush, just in time.

The door opened, and Ranger Smith came out. "Yogi, is that you?" he called, looking cross. Leaving the door opened, Ranger Smith walked away from the Station, trying to see if Yogi was hiding somewhere nearby.

"My plan works!" laughed Yogi, standing up, notching the arrow to the bow, and taking aim.

Twang! The arrow flew through the air. It carried on, through the open door, and landed on the large jam roll on the food table. **Plop!**

"Yah-hay-hay! Bullseye!" cheered Yogi, quickly pulling back the arrow, with the roll attached, with the string.

Without stopping to eat the roll, he fired again. Twang!

Plop! The arrow struck something. Yogi quickly pulled it in. Stuck to the sucker-tip at the end of the arrow was Ranger Smith's nose. Ranger Smith followed closely behind.

"Guuurr! Yogi Bear! I should have known!"

Yogi blushed. "Eeeep! Er, hello, sir! Just practising my archery!"

Ranger Smith dragged Yogi back to his cave. Then he closed the cave entrance with a large boulder. "Now you'll have to stay in there, Yogi! Go back to sleep! I'll see you in the Spring!"

Yogi wasn't happy. "Huh! I'll waste away before then! And with all that lovely grub just waiting to fill me too!"

Then he smiled, and ran to the back of the cave. He pulled up a straw mat to reveal a tunnel running under the ground. "Heh! Ranger Smith doesn't know of my secret escape route in case of emergencies!" With a final chuckle, he crawled into the tunnel...

That evening, the New Year's Eve party was in full swing. The Ranger Station was filled with people in animal fancy dress costumes. One costume especially looked almost life like.

"That's a good costume you're wearing," said a merry Ranger Smith to a 'bear' standing scoffing down the food at the tables. "It reminds me of a pesky bear I have to put up with. But I've tricked him this time – he's trapped in his cave, with no way to escape!"

As the church bells rang in the New Year, the Ranger Smith went off to dance, the guzzling bear grinned happily, and tucked into the food. "Heh! Yogi's no fool, and that's the rule! I'm smarter than the average bear! Heh-heh-hey! Happy New Year!"

THE END

ANSWERS!

Here are the ten monsters that Scooby-Doo spotted. How many did you get?

FROM PAGE 21

R	S	O	M	P	E	B	B	L	E	S	T	F
G	C	L	O	W	S	I	Z	O	F	R	E	D
T	O	T	S	D	I	N	O	N	C	U	E	S
S	O	W	G	M	L	L	P	R	K	B	S	L
R	B	A	M	M	B	A	M	M	W	B	V	A
O	Y	L	D	T	O	P	C	A	T	L	E	T
F	D	E	N	I	O	A	M	B	R	E	L	E
I	O	L	T	N	B	A	R	N	E	Y	M	S
R	O	F	S	W	O	B	R	G	U	T	A	O
G	S	H	A	G	G	Y	L	P	O	J	T	C
A	M	U	T	T	L	E	Y	E	R	O	T	Y

THAT DEVILISH DICK HAS GIVEN YOU ONE WORD TOO MANY! THERE'S NO PENELOPE PITSTOP!

FROM PAGE 34

We managed to find these 35 words in Huckleberry Hound. There's lots more!

LUCK BUCK DUCK ROCK DOCK
BOUND REEK BEER LEER DEER
BUNK ROUND DUNK HURL
CURL BEEN CORK RULE DUEL
ENDURE BLUE CLUE HELD
BOND LEND BEND HERE CURE
LUCKY LOUD KEEN REEL
REEL BURN REBOUND . . .

FROM PAGE 42

ANSWER – BENNY THE BALL.
Benny is missing from the picture.

BYE-BYE EVERYBODY!

FROM PAGE 49